CW01672983

SCOTTISH HIGHLANDS SERIES

ARGYLL
& THE TROSSACHS

David O'Neil

ARGYLL PUBLISHING

First published in 2009 by
Argyll Publishing
Glendaruel
Argyll PA22 3AE
Scotland
www.argyllpublishing.com

**British Library Cataloguing-in-Publication Data.
A catalogue record for this book is available from
the British Library.**

ISBN 978 1 906134 36 5

Printing: Thomson Litho, Glasgow

Contents

Preface	6
From Oban South	7
Seil Island	8
Carnasserie Castle	10
Kilmartin	11
Crinan Canal	13
Lochgilphead	15
Ardrishaig	16
Tarbert	17
South to the Mull	18
Glenbarr Abbey	19
Campbeltown	20
Machrihanish	21
Southend	22
Saddell Castle&Abbey	24
Carradale	25
Arran	27
Lochranza	29
Brodick	30
Lamlash	31
Bute	33
Rothesay	34
Road to the Trossachs	37
Dunoon	37
Loch Lomond West	40
Ardlui	41
Inveruglas	41
Tarbet	43
Inverbeg	44
Luss	44
Balloch	48
The Maid of the Loch	49
Loch Lomond East	50
Balmaha	51
Rowardennan	51
Inversnaid	52
The Trossachs	53
Aberfoyle	54
The Hills and Lochs	55
Loch Katrine	57
Callander	58
Kil, Kin, Aber, Inver	59
The Waters	60
The Clyde Steamers	62
The Puffers	63
The Railways	64

Mull
Glen More
Ben Buie
717
Loch Spelve
Loch Buie
Lochdon
Oban
(An t-Òban)
Kerrera
Firth of Lorn
Connel
Bonawe Quarries
Bonawe
Taynuilt
Ben Cruachan
1126
Lochawe
Loch Nant
Kilchrenan
Dalmally
Glen Orchy
Glen Lochy
Tyndrum
Ben Lui
1130
Crianlarich
(A' Chrion-Làraich)
Ben More
1174
Dochart
Killin
Morenish
Kenknock
Lochay
Ardeor
Lochearnhead
L. Earn
Balquhidder
Kingshouse
Ben Vorlich
985
Loch Voil
Strathyre
Loch Lubnaig
Loch Lomond
& the Trossachs
National Park
Kilninver
Seil
Ellenabeich
Balvicar
Cullipool
Garvellachs
Luing
Sound of Luing
Loch Melfort
Kilmelford
Toberonochy
Cruach Scarba
449
Scarba
Ardfern
Kirkton
Craignish Point
Beinn Chapull
515
Inverinan
Loch Avich
Loch Awe
Cladich
Beinn Bhuidhe
948
Inverarnan
Ardlui
Ben Vorlich
943
Shira
Fyne
Clachan
Cairndow
Beinn Ime
1011
Inveraray Castle
Inveraray
Beinn Bhreac
526
Stronachlachar
Loch Katrine
Ben Ledi
879
Brig o'Turk
Callander
The Trossachs
Loch Venachar
Ford
Kilmartin
Kilmartin House
Auchindrain
Furnace
Newton
Minard
Argyll
Strachur
(Clachan Strachur)
Lochgoilhead
Arrochar
Tarbet
Ben Lomond
974
Kinlochard
Aberfoyle
Port of Menteith
Thornhill
Lake of Menteith
Forth
Queen Elizabeth
Forest Park
Argyll Forest Park
Invernoaden
Loch Eck
Loch Goil
Loch Long
Doune Hill
734
Luss
Loch Lomond
Balmaha
Arnprior
Kippen
Buchlyvie
Balfron
Gargunnock Hills
Fintry
Crinan
Bridgend
Cairnbaan
Lochgilphead
Beinn Bhreac
467
Jura
Ardlussa
Tayvallich
Ardrishaig
Loch Gilp
Loch Fyne
Otter Ferry
Glendaruel
Clachan of Glendaruel
Beinn Mhor
742
Ardentinny
Cnoc a' Mhadaidh
470
Garelochhead
Coulport
Gare Loch
Cove
Kilcreggan
Rhu
Helensburgh
Arden
Gartocharn
Drymen
Killearn
Earl's Seat
578
Campsie
Meikle Bin
570
Fells
Craighat
Balloch
Alexandria
Strathblane
Lennoxtown
Milton of Campsie
Mugdock Country Park
Kilpatrick Hills
Dumbarton
Milngavie
Torrance
Bearsden
Bishopbriggs
Kirkintilloch
Clydebank
Sound of Jura
Tarbert
Keillmore
Loch Sween
Achahoish
Danna Island
Kilmory
Inverneill
Knapdale
Kilfinan
Craigandaive
Auchenbreck
Beinn Bhreac
507
Colintraive
Port Driseach
Tighnabruaich
Kames
Millhouse
Strone
Hunter's Quay
Dunoon
Innellan
Gourock
Greenock
Craigendoran
Cardross
Port Glasgow
Kilmacolm
Bishopton
Clyde
A82
A85
A816
A819
A83
A84
A81
A821
A873
A811
A875
A809
A891
A814
A817
A818
A815
A880
A886
A8003
A78
A770
A846
A849
M8
B8077
B8074
B845
B840
B844
B8003
B8002
B8025
B841
B8000
B8024
B828
B839
B829
B836
B833
B822
B835
B818
B8034
B826
B8048
A879

Kilberry
Kennacraig
West Loch Tarbert
Ardpatrick Point
Skipness
Clachan
Claonaig
Sound of Bute
Ardlamont Point
Meikle Kilmory
Kingarth
Great Cumbrae
Millport
Little Cumbrae
Firth of
Largs
Fairlie
Gigha
Ballochroy
Crossaig
Cock of Arran
Lochranza
Garroch Head
Ardminish
Sound of Gigha
Tayinloan
Killean
Cara Island
Kintyre
Caisteal Abhail 859
Pirnmill
Corrie
Goat Fell 874
BRODICK CASTLE & GARDEN
Kilbrannan Sound
Carradale
Beinn an Tuirc 454
Dougarie
Arran
Brodick
Glenacardoch Point
Glenbarr
Dippen
Ard Bheinn 512
Bellochantuy Bay
Saddell
Tormore
Lamlash
Lussa Loch
Blackwaterfoot
Whiting Bay
Kilchenzie
Campbeltown
Peninver
Ardnacross Bay
Machrihanish Bay
Davaar Island
Lagg
Bennan Head
Pladda
Machrihanish
Campbeltown (Ceann Loch Chille Chiarain)
Cnoc Moy 446
Conie Glen
Feochaig
Southend
Macharioch
Mull of Kintyre
Sanda Island
Ailsa Craig
Portencross
Seamill
West Kilbride
Ardrossan
Saltcoats
Stevenston
Irvine
Irvine Bay
Barassie
Troon
Prestwick
Glasgow Prestwick
Ayr
Heads of Ayr
Dunure
Brown Carrick Hill 287
Culzean Bay
CULZEAN COUNTRY PARK & CASTLE
Maidens
Turnberry
Girvan
Larne (summer only)
(winter only)
(summer only)
Hill of Stake 522
CASTLE SEMPLE COUNTRY PARK
Johnstone
Paisley
GLENIFFER BRAES C. PARK
Howwood
Lochwinnoch
Barrhead
Neilston
Newton Mearns
Giffnock
Rutherglen
Uddingston
High Blantyre
East Kilbride
CALDERGLEN COUNTRY PARK
Kilbirnie
Beith
Hall
Glengarnock
Burnhouse
Dunlop
Eaglesham
Dalry
Stewarton
Coarse Hill
Strathaven
Kilwinning
Fenwick
Kilmaurs
Moscow
Springside
Kilmarnock
Darvel
Drumclog
Dreghorn
Crosshouse
Hurlford
Newmilns
Galston
Dundonald
Symington
Loans
Crosshands
Mauchline
Muirkirk
Tarbolton
Catrine
Sorn
Mossblown
Annbank
Auchinleck
Ochiltree
Cumnock
Logan
Alloway
Coylton
Drongan
Hollybush
Littlemill
Dalrymple
New Cumnock
Patna
Kirkmichael
Maybole
Kirkoswald
Crosshill
Dalmellington
Enoch Hill 569
Blackcraig Hill 700
Craigdarroch
Dailly
Old Dailly
Cairnsmore of Carsphairn 797
Loch Doon
Ayr
Annick
A83
A78
A737
A726
A761
A760
A736
A735
A77
A719
A71
A76
A70
A79
A713
A841
A844
M77
B8024
B8001
B842
B843
B880
B881
B896
B776
B775
B771
B706
B780
B714
B778
B769
B764
B743
B744
B7037
B730
B705
B7046
B7024
B742
B7045
B741

Preface

IN THIS the third book in the Scottish Highland Series, once again I have tried to describe the area simply, leaving the reader the choice to explore in more detail. The area covered is one of the prettiest to be found in Scotland and an area that has had a major impact on the forming of the Scottish nation.

I have not included the Atlantic Islands as I consider them more suitably covered in a dedicated book of the Hebrides, forthcoming in the series.

David O'Neil
February 2009

From Oban to the South

HEADING SOUTH from Oban the A816 road first climbs over Soroba hill before winding its way through the green, tree scattered countryside. Up and down hills with occasional flashes of the blue waters of the Atlantic on the right. Offshore the island of Kerrera looms. At Kilmore the road is joined by the old road that links the network of drove roads that cross the hills from Connel, through Glen Cruitten, round the east of Oban past Loch Nell (which translates as Swan Lake!).

These roads are all single track and if you intend to explore them, make sure your reversing skills are up to scratch.

North Pier, Oban

Seil Island and the Bridge

FROM KILMORE the A816 runs alongside Loch Feochan, to Kilninver, which is the turn-off to Seil Island and Easdale Island (famous for slate production in the nineteenth and early twentieth centuries). Taking this diversion is most rewarding as the narrow road is picturesque and it entails crossing the famous bridge over the Atlantic, a Telford bridge that literally crosses an arm of the sea to reach Seil Island.

Follow the signs on the island for Easdale. From the viewpoint above Ellanbeich can be seen the island of Easdale and the scattering of islands to the south, with the bulk of Jura looming large. Away to the west the tail end of Mull and perhaps a distant glimpse of the Isle of Colonsay.

Ellanbeich (Little Island) is an odd name for a village on the mainland. The village was once on an island, the gap between island and mainland was filled but the name remained. Basically the ferry point for Easdale, it has toilets, a general store and restaurant; there is also the headquarters of the Highland Arts chain of shops, complete with an art gallery dedicated to the work of C. John Taylor, founder of the business. Just before reaching the village proper the garden of An Cala House is open to the public during the spring and summer.

Highland Arts. Easdale Tel: 01852 300273
An Cala Gardens. Easdale Tel: 01852 300237

Bridge over the Atlantic

The main road continues south to Kilmelford, a small loch-side community, known for its sheltered moorings that can be seen offshore along the sheltered inlet from the Atlantic Ocean. The Princess Royal has been known to moor her yacht here; this modern development includes timeshare, self-catering and hotel accommodation.

Following the shores of Loch Melfort the road takes a sharp turn to the left, along the coast. On the bend is another popular garden, run by the National Trust for Scotland, Arduaine Gardens. The gardens run down to the shore and overlook the sea and the islands of Luing and Shuna. The area from this point becomes increasingly interesting historically.

Carnasserie Castle

Carnasserie Castle

ON THE RIGHT above the road stands the ruin of sixteenth century Carnasserie Castle one-time home of Bishop John Carswell, who translated John Knox's book of Common Order into Gaelic.

A tower house castle of the period with an adjoining hall house, it has three carved panels over the door depicting the arms of God, King and Campbell, and the interior was supplied with water to the kitchen through the wall from outside using a stone water channel.

The countryside from here south becomes increasingly pleasant. Though there are still low hills the ground tends to level down and the views become more open.

Kilmartin

Kilmartin Church

WITHIN two miles of Carnasserie the road reaches Kilmartin, a centre of great historical and cultural significance. Kilmartin Glen is full of cairns, standing stones and a Bronze Age linear cemetery. In addition the church has an exhibition of gravestones dating from the Middle Ages, among which can found evidence of the presence of the Knights Templar.

There is a Heritage Centre with a museum of great interest with a fine cafe/restaurant. As is so often the case the village pub, the Kilmartin Hotel is conveniently opposite the Church.

Kilmartin House Tel : 01546 510278
The Kilmartin Hotel Tel : 01546510250

Standing Stones

From here on can be seen standing stones away to the right, and the important site of Dunadd, one time seat of the fifth century Scottish kingdom of Dalriada can be reached along a short side road. It is possible to climb the Dun, the track being signposted, and though the original 'footprint' in the rock on the summit has been removed a replica has been placed in situ, The history of the site is believed to be much older than Dalriada and it is regarded as a significant site of much more ancient times.

From here it is a short drive to Cairnbaan, which stands close to the summit level of the Crinan Canal. There are cup- and ring-marked rocks some 200 yards north of the Cairnbaan Hotel, which stands beside the canal at this point.

Cairnbaan Hotel Tel: 01546 603668

Crinan Canal

Crinan Harbour

THE LITTLE harbour at Crinan is protected from the Atlantic by sea lock gates. The Canal comes into the harbour from Crinan Loch. Just a tiny village on the edge of the land, it provides shelter and accommodation and a doorway into the sea beyond. The Crinan Hotel stands beside the harbour and has a reputation for seafood.

By land the large rock behind which the village shelters is known as MacDonald's Seat. The road beside the Canal goes round the opposite side of the rock to meet the canal once more at the harbour.

As can be seen from maps of the area, the Crinan Canal is only 8.5 miles long running from Ardrishaig to Crinan on the Atlantic coast. The 17 locks raise the level about 64 feet, and at one time this canal was an important link for travellers sailing to and up the west coast to Oban and beyond. To travel round the Mull of Kintyre to reach Crinan meant a sea voyage of 130 miles. Built for private investors in the late eighteenth century by John Rennie, its importance was enhanced when the Caledonian Canal opened, as it allowed easier access to northern waters for Clyde and Loch Fyne fishing boats. Still much in use by yacht and fishing craft, the canal plays host through the winter to the last surviving steam puffers, *Vic 32*, now carrying holiday makers round the coasts, and sometime the sadly neglected *Vital Spark* (Auld Reekie) refitted for use in the TV Series. Now re-named *The Maggie* it is in process of being moved to Inveraray for refit and exhibition. The B841 from Cairnbaan, parallels the canal, and is suitable for car traffic; there is a car park alongside the canal basin at Crinan.

Back on the A816 it is just a few minutes to the town of Lochgilphead.

The Crinan Hotel Tel: 01546 603210

Lochgilphead

STANDING as it does at the north end of Kintyre, Lochgilphead occupies a strategic position. At the junction of the Inveraray-Oban-Campbelltown road roughly halfway between Oban and Campbelltown, the Crinan Canal runs into Loch Gilp approximately two miles south of the town.

The principal administrative offices of Argyll & Bute Council are housed at the site of Kilmory Castle which lies on the Inveraray Road, at the east end of town. The castle grounds contain a Victorian walled garden, open to the public, which has been restored to its former glory over the last few years. There is also a visitor and information centre within the grounds with special reference to the trees to be found within the precincts.

Once the terminus for the Clyde steamers, and a transfer point for passengers travelling onwards through the Crinan Canal, Lochgilphead is now a quiet corner of a beautiful area belying its once bustling past.

Kilmory Woodland Park Tel: 01546 602127

Ardrishaig

FROM Lochgilphead down the A83 southwards is the eastern end of the Crinan Canal, at Ardrishaig, a centre for West Coast Motors (the bus company covering most of Argyll), a small group of shops, and the Locks from the Canal into the waters of Loch Gilp. Just south of this little village the road forks right to the Knapdale hills where trail riding and clay pigeon shooting is available at the riding centre.

Argyll Trail Riding Centre Tel: 01546 603274

Tarbert

Tarbert and the way south

The town of Tarbert lies 14 miles south down Loch Fyne on the eastern side of Kintyre. It is overlooked by the ruined castle on the hill above the little town on the inner shore of East Loch Tarbert.

The name dates from the time when Vikings claimed all the islands down the coast of Scotland. Kintyre was claimed by trickery. The ships sailed from Tarbert, round the Mull to West Loch Tarbert, where the ships were lifted and carried over the isthmus to East Loch Tarbert, apparently without dropping their sails. The distance was perhaps two miles. A Tarbet or Tarbert is a place of easy portage across the land. There are several places so named in Scotland.

The harbour provides a safe anchorage and is much used by yachts and cruisers sailing the waters of the Firth of Clyde and surrounding lochs. Many boats are based in the moorings beside the town, and there is a ferry port linked to Portavadie on the other side of Loch Fyne, and Lochranza on the Isle of Arran.

B&B and hotel Accommodation is available in the area. In town the Tarbert Hotel is on the waterfront. Three miles north of town, Stonefield Castle Hotel, with its 60 acres of woodland gardens is situated on the lochside, providing stunning views and comfortable accommodation.

Tarbert Castle, though now a ruin, was rebuilt about

1325 by order of Robert the Bruce because of its strategic situation. It is believed to be constructed on the site of a Roman fort. The town has an art gallery and several restaurants, a golf course and riding stables.

Stonefield Castle Hotel Tel: 01880 820836
Loch Fyne Gallery Tel: 0880 820390
Highland Horse Riding Tel: 01880 820333
Barra Gall Craft Shop Tel: 01880 820428

South to the Mull

The A83 continues south via West Loch Tarbert past the ferry port of Kennacraig. From here passage can be taken to the islands of Jura and Islay.

The view opens out beyond the confines of the loch as the coast turns south. At Clachan is a village shop and petrol station and west of the village is the hill fort of Dun Skeig. Clachan was the home of the church in north Kintyre. Nearby Loup Hill was the scene, where in the eighteenth century the last major battle in Kintyre was fought. Three local Jacobite chieftains met defeat at the hands of government forces.

Ronachan Point is a good viewpoint overlooking the Sounds of Gigha and Jura, the offshore islands silhouetted against the horizon to the west. It is also the site of the bloody Dunaverty Massacre of 1647 which followed the razing of Largie Castle.

Further south the village of Tayinloan is the ferry point for the island of Gigha.

The sign Glenbarr Abbey points inland to the home of the Macalisters of Glenbarr. The house is eighteenth century and it contains a collection of nineteenth century fashions and jewelry. A pair of gloves worn by Mary Queen of Scots form part of the collection.

Glenbarr Abbey

GLENBARR Abbey is open to the public during the summer and tours are conducted by members of the family. The grounds have woodland walks, a museum a café and gift shop. Access to Beinn an Tuirc (454m) the highest hill in Kintyre, can be gained from the road past the Abbey.

At Bellochantuy Bay the beach conditions are favourable for surfing.

A few miles south the road turns inland away from the sea across the peninsula to Campbeltown.

Glenbarr Visitor Centre Tel: 01583 421247

Campbeltown

THE BIGGEST settlement on Kintyre was once known as Kinlochkerran – its charter dates back to Robert the Bruce. During the period of the Stuart kings the burgh was granted to the Campbells of Argyll and the name was changed in their honour. The main business of the town was fishing and distilling, the loch beside the town giving name to the traditional drinking song 'Campbeltown Loch'. Sadly the fishing industry has declined though the Springbank distillery is still open offering tours to visitors. The island of Davaar lies at the seaward end of the loch, and there can be found the lighthouse and caves in one of which can be seen a painting of the crucifixion by Archibald Mackinnon.

St.Kiaran visited the area from Ireland before Columba came to Scotland and he gave his name to the settlement. St Kiaran's Cave is on the shore three miles south. A fifteenth century Celtic Cross stands at the Old Quay Head. There is golf, sea fishing and sailing, and the interesting historic country around the town makes it worth the visit.

Springbank Distillery Tel: 01586 552085
The Ardshiel Hotel Tel: 01586 552133

Campbeltown

Machrihanish

SIX MILES from Campbeltown on the West coast the one-time salt and coal producing area round Machrihanish later became famous for its airfield and is now popular for its golf course and over three miles of sandy beach on the Atlantic coast.

In the past, coal was produced at Drumlemble two miles east of the village. Originally shipped by canal to Campbeltown, a light railway was installed to replace the canal service; this was later extended to Machrihanish and was used extensively to carry day trippers from Glasgow who had arrived by steamer. In 1932 the mine closed and by 1933 the railway was closed. A bus service replaced the train subsequently.

Southend

At the very end of the Mull, Southend is where St Columba first set foot in Scotland. A flat rock below the ruined chapel is believed to be where he landed on his first mission here. From the village the road runs round the shore past the Island of Sanda with its lighthouse. Against the rock face on the land side of the road the ruin of an Art Deco Hotel stands next to the burnt-out ruin of Kiel Point School. The ruin of the chapel is next in line under the cliff. A religious service is held in June each year in the chapel.

Little remains of the ruin of Dunaverty Castle once held by the Lord of the Isles. Captured by James IV in 1493, it was again captured by Leslie in 1647 when the entire garrison was put to the sword.

St Columba's Churchyard

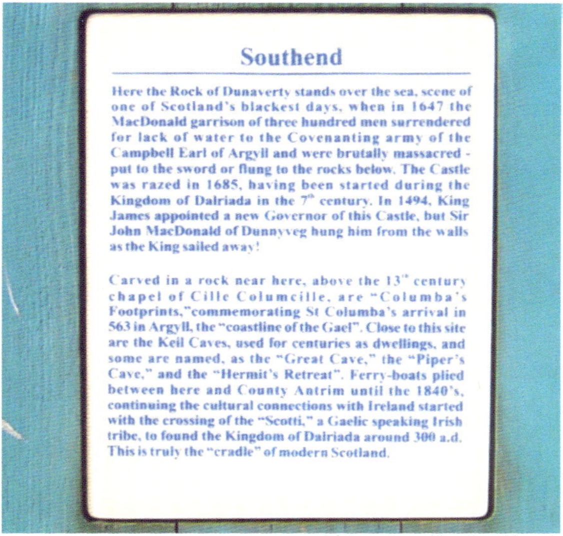

History Board by the Church

The road continues for just over six miles to the Mull of Kintyre lighthouse located on the Atlantic side of the point. It is possible to drive to a small car park above the

Mull of Kintyre Lighthouse

lighthouse, where a path drops down the steep rock to the lighthouse below.

From the car park Ireland is clearly visible thirteen miles away. The road north is through Campbelltown and up the east side of the peninsula on the B842.

Saddell Castle & Abbey

SADDELL Bay is about eight miles north along the B842. The castle that stands above the bay dates from 1508 though little is known about it. It is believed to stand on the site of an earlier castle built by Somerled when he was Lord of the Isles in the twelfth century. The ruined Abbey dates from this time and is also believed to have been built by Somerled.

The castle has been restored and upgraded and is now divided into a series of privately occupied apartments. The abbey ruins are open to the public and they contain several early carvings.

Carradale

CARRADALE Bay is a nicely sheltered bay facing across the Kilbrannan Sound to Arran.Once a fishing port with a harbour built in 1959, it is now mainly devoted to sailing and cruising boats. On the Point which embraces Carradale Bay to the south, is a vitrified fort.

Within the village, now mainly concerned with holidays, there is a gold/silversmith, a heritage centre and tearoom, and Torrisdale Castle, which provides a tannery and self-catering accommodation both in the nineteenth century castle as well as in cottages within the extensive grounds. There is a local golf course and hotels.

Network Carradale Heritage Centre Tel: 10583 431296
Torrisdale Castle Tannery Tel: 01583 431233
Carradale Gold Foundry Tel: 01583 431683

To Claonaig, Skipness and Tarbert the road along the coast north overlooks the Isle of Arran across Kilbrannan Sound. At Claonaid the ferry operates to Lochranza on the Isle of Arran (30 mins).

At Claonaid the road off to the right is the B8001 to Skipness point. The thirteenth century Skipness Castle is located at the point beyond the village and is open to the public. The castle marked the southern boundary of Campbell territory.

Kilbrannan Chapel which dates from the thirteenth

century was built to replace St Columba's Chapel on the same site. It stands by the shore below Skipness Castle. It is cared for by Historic Scotland as is the castle ruin.

The road back to Tarbert crosses the peninsula once more to Kennacraig, thence to Tarbert.

Skipness Castle

Arran

Of all the Scottish sslands Arran must be one of the most photographed and painted. A landscape of sea-washed shores and high towering mountains 21.5 miles long by 9 miles wide. Rising from the waters of the Firth of Clyde, for over a century it has been a favoured holiday resort for the people of Glasgow and the south of Scotland. The beauty of the landscape that has so captivated visitors is largely unspoilt and though the island has experienced expansion in the building of houses, efforts have been made to restrict inappropriate development.

Hen Harrier

In addition, with the modern attitude to conservation, wildlife is being respected and protected with formerly lost species such as the hen harrier returning to the island during the 1950s. Ferry access to the island is from Claonaig on Kintyre, and Ardrossan on the Ayrshire coast.

Historically Arran has figured in important events. The fleet of the Norse King Haakon anchored in the shelter of Arran in 1263.The weather was foul and his ships scattered. From there he decided to attack the Scottish army camped across the Firth at Largs. His attack was made at night when he hoped the Scottish army would asleep, especially in the dark and stormy conditions. His men crept through the heather apparently barefoot so as not to disturb the sleeping Scots. Thistles in among the heather caused several of the Vikings to cry out, wakening the sleeping Scots, who promptly rose and fought the attacking Norsemen. The result was defeat for King Haakon and his men and eventually the end of the Norse control of the Western Isles. King Haakon was injured and died of his wounds in Kirkwall, Orkney whilst on the return journey to Norway.

Legend has it that from this time onwards the thistle became part of the Scottish insignia.

Lochranza

Lochranza

The village tucked into the corner of the hills at the head of the loch has been in being for centuries. The castle on the gravel spit dates from the thirteenth century currently maintained by Historic Scotland, last owned by the Duke of Hamilton. In its chequered career the castle has seen Robert the Bruce on his return from Ireland prior to assuming the crown of Scotland. James 1 of Scotland used it as a base against the Lord of the Isles, and James VI used it as a hunting lodge. Maintained until the end of the eighteenth century, it has fallen into disuse since.

The distillery has been operating since 1995; the visitor centre was opened by the Queen in 1997. There is a golf course and plenty of accommodation available. The castle itself was believed to have been the inspiration for the castle in the Tintin adventure 'The Black Isle'.

The Island of Arran has a perimeter road, the A841 around the shoreline. Departing from Lochranza towards Brodick, the main town, the road rises over a ridge to reveal a stunning view of the mountains rising to Goat Fell (2868 ft), the most prominent of the Arran peaks. Across the Firth the low lying shore of the mainland forms a background to the restless water. The little village of Corrie, with two tiny harbours lies stretched along the shoreline. With a pretty location and a hotel, this little village causes many travellers to drag their feet. A short five miles down the road Brodick Bay lies embracing the Castle and village.

Brodick Castle

Brodick

The largest community on the island, served by ferry from Ardrossan, Brodick is a favoured destination for holiday makers. The Bay is overlooked from the north by Brodick Castle, and the only tourist office on the island is right opposite the quay.

At the eastern end of the bay lies the little harbour. A heritage museum provides background information and intimate detail of the island's turbulent history. Having been occupied by Vikings until the eleventh century and several different clan and government troop occupations since, the museum has plenty of variety to offer.

The castle is open to the public with extensive grounds and a visitor centre. It dates from the original thirteenth century castle built by the Stewarts of Menteith, though during its chequered career, other owners have included HenryVIII and Cromwell. Alterations to the building carried out at various times led to its conversion from a stronghold to its present form as a stately family home. Property of the Dukes of Hamilton, its last conversion was in 1844, but it is of interest that during repairs in 1977 an unknown staircase was discovered leading to a forgotten room within the walls of the castle. It is also haunted but this does not detract from the beautiful interior of this glorious home.

Brodick Castle Tel: 01770 860466

Lamlash

Lamlash Church

The road passes through the village of Lamlash that lies towards the southern end of Arran. Its position opposite the Holy Isle makes it the most popular anchorage for yachting enthusiasts, with good mooring and chandlery facilities.

Recent actions by conservationists has caused the bay to be placed under a 'no fishing' order to preserve the scallop beds for posterity.

Once Lamlash vied with Brodick as the ferry port for the island, now despite the fact it is smaller than Brodick it is still important as the site of the main hospital and local government offices. The golf course has wonderful views over Holy Island.

This small rocky island off Arran is owned by Buddhist monks who have a retreat on the island. The peak, Mullach Mor is over 1000 ft. A ferry takes visitors to the island for the walks and the climbs. Dogs, alcohol and fires are not permitted.

Back on Arran there are other small settlements on the road round the island, beautiful scenery and a wealth of history waiting to be discovered. At Blackwaterfoot the B860 joins the ring road. The so called 'String' road crosses the island from Brodick through the mountains, passing stone circles and a burial chamber at Balmichael, three miles from Blackwaterfoot. The circuit of the island is about 56 miles, with a population of about 4500. Although many people just visit for the day, the island merits a longer stay to take in its full range of sights and interests.

Rothesay Harbour

Bute

The Isle of Bute lies in Firth of Clyde separated from the Cowal peninsula by the Kyles. It is served by ferries from Wemyss Bay to Rothesay and across the Kyles of Bute, from Colintrave to Rhubodach at the north of the island.

Fifteen miles by five miles, this small island has been a focus for the holidaymakers from the Glasgow area for a major part of the nineteenth and twentieth centuries. The legendary Clyde steamers contested for a place at the piers of Rothsay throughout the summer, the saying 'Doon the Watter' truly meaning a trip to Rothesay even if it extended through the Kyles of Bute and down to Arran.

Glasgow Fair weeks were the climax of the season, when the factories of the city all received their annual holidays. The clyde steamers were operated privately from various Clydeside ports. Ships operated by the railway company entered the competition when the rail link to Wemyss Bay was completed in 1886.

Speed on the water was always regarded as important since for many the trip to Rothesay was a day trip. Day trippers booked on the fastest boats. The piers at Rothesay saw physical violence on occasion between rival ships. (see The Waters)

Rothesay

The capital of the island is known for its Winter Gardens now housing the Discovery Centre and the imposing Victorian toilets on the pier. In the centre of town stands the thirteenth century castle, scene of many battles since it was first constructed by Alan, Steward to William I. The museum has records of the history of Bute and of the surrounding area.

Rothesay itself has passed through many stages, as a stronghold, and later as a fishing port once home to approximately 80 herring boats. And in the twentieth century as a holiday resort with the second busiest harbour on the Clyde.

Whilst the halcyon days of the steamer trade are long gone, tourism continues. The ease of access to the area still gives it a deserved popularity as a holiday resort, with its hotels and guest houses and the many attractions.

Other places of interest on the island are Port Bannatyne which lies 1.5 miles north of Rothesay on the A886. This village has been regarded as the quiet alternative to Rothesay since its development in 1900. Little has been done to it since and it remains the pleasant little place with the best beach on the island. It also features a shipwreck which has become a feature of the village.

Greenfinch

The local 18-hole golf course adds to the attraction of this pleasant spot, which features a fourteenth century castle at the head of Kames Bay on which Port Bannatyne stands. From Port Bannatyne the road continues to the north of Bute to end at the ferry point to Colintrave.

The southern part of the island is served by the A844 which you can drive to the southern village of Kingarth standing on Kilchattan Bay.

Mount Stuart, the seat of the Marquess of Bute, is a

major international atttraction and at Kingarth is a riding and trekking centre.

Bute is surrounded by beautiful green hilly country rising to craggy mountains. The waters around are often dotted with sails from the many boats kept in and around the shores.

Benmore Pines

The Road to the Trossachs

From the Colintrave ferry travel north on the A886 with the Kyles of Bute and Loch Riddon on your left. Turn right at the junction onto the single track B836 to Dunoon. Follow this narrow road through the hills past the head of Loch Striven then through Glen Lean. The road runs to the head of the Holy Loch, where, the US Naval Base was once established. It joins the A815 to Dunoon.

Dunoon

Dunoon

The town of Dunoon was once one of the important destinations on the Clyde. Very much part of the 'Doon the Watter' experience, the Hotels and B&Bs in this waterside location accessed from the river were as popular a destination as Rothesay or Helensburgh.

The town prospered during the golden years of the Clyde steamers with the beautiful hills of Argyll as a backdrop. Sadly with the passing of this era, the tourism declined and despite the rise of the coach traffic, the town has never really regained the popularity it once enjoyed.

Dunoon is however still packed every year for the Cowal Highland Games. Said to be the biggest Games in Scotland, Cowal is famous for the pipe band competition that draws entries from across the world. The climax of the games involves a march through the town by up to one hundred competing bands.

Connected by ferry to Gourock with swift access to Glasgow by rail or car, a second ferry also runs from neighbouring Hunters Quay.

CalMac Ferries Dunoon.Tel: 01369 706491
Western Ferries. Dunoon.Tel: 01369 704452

The road to Glasgow overland is a much more extensive undertaking. The A 815 North runs north past the head of the Holy Loch to Benmore Botanic Gardens, a beautifully located garden with a backdrop of Redwood trees. A visitor centre with café and exhibition is on this spectacular botanical site.

Behind the garden is the Benmore Centre for outdoor education which provides facilities for youth training in outdoor activity. Residential courses are held on a range of activities from canoeing to hill climbing.

Benmore Botanic Garden Tel: 01369 706261
Benmore Centre Tel: 01369 706337

The road continues north along the precipitous edge of Loch Eck to Strachur on Loch Fyne. The town of Inveraray can be seen across the loch as the road nears the junction with the A83.

At the junction turn right and almost immediately

the road climbs up through Glen Kinglas and over the the 'Rest and be Thankful' pass. A viewpoint has been constructed at the hill top giving the spectacular view down the famous stretch of road. No longer as steep, the new road has cut out much of the notorious switchback that once caused consternation to the unwary motorist. Sections of the old road are still visible below the new.

The descent downhill runs through a fold in the mountains with Ben Lochan on the right rising to over 2000 ft. To the left 'The Cobbler' rises 2891 ft. Better seen from the other direction, this is one of the most famous mountains of this clutch of peaks known as the Arrochar Alps.

Around the head of Loch Long the road forks – down the eastern shore of the loch is the direct route to Helensburgh via Garelochhead; straight on the road continues to Loch Lomond at Tarbet.

Loch Lomond Western Shore

The western shore of Loch Lomond is bordered by the main road north, A 82, for about 16 miles. At the head of the Loch is Inverarnan which is distinguished by the Drovers Inn on the right of the road and the Drovers Lodge on the left.

The Drovers Inn was established 300 years ago on the Cattle drove road beside Loch Lomond. Considering the location of the inn and its links with cattle movements, it is likely that Rob Roy the cattle trader, and later General Wade's road builders, or indeed the General himself and many of their contemporaries would have used the Inn!

Providing food, drink and accommodation this interesting historic building is a focus for visitors. From north to south the features of the Loch reflect the history and economics of this part of Scotland.

Within the woods can be found both pine martens and red squirrels.

Drovers Inn Inverarnan Tel: 01301 704234

Ardlui

Just down the road at Ardlui, there is a hotel and marina, a camping and caravan site and a railway station. The shore of the narrow northern section of Loch Lomond is served by cruise boats and a ferry to the opposite side of the loch to link up with the West Highland Way. There are several mapped walks that can be taken from the village and there is also a bird centre at the north end of the railway station.

Serious climbers can take some challenging routes over the slopes of Ben Vorlich to Sloy and Inveruglas.

Ardlui Hotel and Marina Tel: 0131 04243

Inveruglas

At Inveruglas, the Sloy hydro scheme is a pumped storage power station similar to Cruachan on the shores of Loch Awe; the waters come through a three mile tunnel from Loch Vorlich.

Ben Lomond

The waters of Loch Vorlich are enhanced through a series of tunnels and an aqueduct from both north and south enlarging the natural catchment area. In addition water is pumped up at night from Loch Lomond to reinforce the supply.

Opposite the power station the picnic area and toilets are sited beside a car park and jetty used by Cruise Loch Lomond boats who run scenic trips and ferry journeys throughout the summer. There is also a visitor centre and café on the site.

The road from Inverarnan through Ardlui and Inveruglas to Tarbet is narrow and twisting. Extra care should be taken driving on this stretch of road especially when meeting coaches and large lorries as there are several places where passing can be difficult.

Tarbet

Historically Tarbet is the place where in 1263, Viking raiders dragged their boats from the head of Loch Long (sea loch) to the fresh waters of Loch Lomond. The 1.5 mile transit proved no obstacle. They were able to launch their boats and plunder both sides of the loch and the inhabited islands believed up to that time to be secure from attack.

Although a small village Tarbet has the Tarbet Hotel that stands at the junction of the A82/A83 and just up the A83 towards Arrochar, a tearoom and an interesting craft shop.

Located just thirty miles from Glasgow with road and rail links, Tarbet makes a convenient centre for walking touring and sailing, surrounded as it is with stunning scenery.

Tarbet Hotel Tel: 01301 702346
Cruise Loch Lomond Tel: 01301 702356

Inverbeg

Southwards where Glen Douglas runs down to the shore, the hamlet of Inverbeg is dominated by the Inverbeg Inn. Recently refurbished standing above the road on the west side backing onto the mountain slopes, the hotel offers a warm welcoming appearance.

In Glen Douglas itself, just off the road is the Inverbeg galleries. Known for its wide selection of Scottish artists the gallery has been in existence for over forty years in its present location.

A small ferry runs through the summer season to Rowardennan on the east shore of the Loch

Inverbeg Inn Tel: 01436 860678
Inverbeg Galleries Tel: 01436 860277

Luss

Perhaps the most famous of the villages on this road the village of Luss has been the watering place for coach tours, boat cruises and Glasgow trippers from the 1930s to the present day. Dating back at least a thousand years the village was once a milling and slate mining centre. It is famous in Scotland through its association with the long-runnong TV series 'Take the High Road'.

A Viking gravestone can be seen in the churchyard.

The Pier at Luss

Other stones can be seen dating from the seventh and eighth centuries. A National Park centre is located at the car park, with toilets and there is a general store and milk bar.

The area is Colquhoun country, the lands infamous for the bloody battle of nearby Glen Fruin. In 1603, two hundred MacGregor men left Luss having come to negotiate friendly terms. After leaving to return north via Glen Fruin they were followed by Colquhoun who was obviously unhappy with the outcome.

Suspecting treachery MacGregor split his men into two parties of 100, sending his deputy with 100 men to swing round behind the hills to defend his rear. With 500 men the Colquhoun chieftain attacked MacGregor in Glen Fruin, but they were taken by surprise from the rear by Macgregor's rearguard. Two hundred Colquhouns were killed.

Unfortunately many onlookers who had attended the

peace talks including several Burgesses of Dumbarton who had followed Colquhoun to Glen Fruin were also killed.

The resultant indignation and representations made to King James was the reason he decided to proscribe the entire Clan Gregor. Any man using the name could be put to death instantly. The renowned Rob Roy was therefore known for years as Rob Roy Campbell (his mother's name).

The Luss Highland Games are held annually on the field beside the old loop road, once the main road, which runs past the car park. To the north of the car park stands the Lodge on the Loch Hotel with magnificent views.

Lodge on the Loch Hotel Tel: 01436 860201
Highland Arts. Luss Tel: 01436 860233
National Park Centre Tel: 01389 722120
Coach House Coffee Shop Tel: 01463 860341

Although technically still part of Luss the Loch Lomond Golf Club has an international competition standard course; completed comparatively recently it has already hosted several major events. The course lies between the road and the waters of the loch and is very picturesque

The Carrick course was completed in 2007. Owned by the DeVere Cameron House Hotel it promises ample golfing facilities within the Loch Lomond area. This course is open to the public

Loch Lomond Golf Club Tel: 01436 655555
DeVere Cameron House Hotel Tel: 01389 755565

The River Leven, Balloch

The roundabout at Arden, opposite the grounds of the Carrick golf course marks the point where the B831/2 from Helensburgh joins the A82, the inland link road to Glasgow. From here the A82 continues south past the grounds, on the left, of the DeVere Cameron Hotel to the loop road to the Duck Bay marina and hotel.

The marina jetty is a popular boating departure point and a centre for leisure sailing on Loch Lomond. A large picnic area and car park attract weekend crowds from Glasgow and the surrounding area. Opposite Duck Bay on the west side of the road the magnificent Victorian mansion that is a Youth Hostel attracts the eye.

About one mile south of Duck Bay the Balloch roundabout marks the point where a left turn onto the A811 takes the traveller in the direction of the Trossachs.

Balloch

The village of Balloch lies at the south end of Loch Lomond across the mouth of the River Leven. It is dedicated mainly to the operation and care of the boating fraternity and many of the cruise boats in the southern part of the Loch depart from here.

The village has a variety of small shops linked to supply and service of the boating public, with restaurants and hotel accommodation and chandlery.

It retains its charm despite the bustle of modern life. The west end of the village has seen the development of Loch Lomond Shores, a new development, with a department store, a marine exhibition in a specially constructed exhibition hall and a variety of smaller shops to attract holiday traffic, all located on the southern shore of Loch Lomond.

The Maid of the Loch

Moored alongside the public slipway beside Loch Lomond Shores, the *Maid of the Loch* has been permanently based here for many years. The reconstruction and the refurbishment of this historic steam ship has been a triumph for the committee of amateurs who love the thought of sailing the waters of Loch Lomond on a paddle steamer once more. The restoration work is being carried out by volunteers giving up their time to paint and chip rust every weekend.

The dining area has been refurbished and private functions are held to help with the fundraising for the eventual final restoration to bring the ship back into service.

Maid of the Loch Bookings Tel: 01389 710138

The River Leven connects Loch Lomond with the River Clyde. Just south of Balloch the town of Alexandria, once home of the Argyll Car manufacturing company, now known for its outlets located in the old Argyll factory, and Antartex, the woollen mill complex, hosts coach parties the year round.

Loch Lomond Eastern Shore

The largest expanse of fresh water on the mainland of Britain, Loch Lomond is 24 miles long, 5 miles wide and 600 feet deep.

There are 38 islands including Inchmurrin which has a hotel. The loch is the part of the Loch Lomond National Park, the first to be established in Scotland.

The main road north A82 runs the full length of the loch on the western bank. On the eastern shore is the famous West Highland Way, created in the eighteenth century by General Wade as a military road and currently walked by thousands of enthusiasts every year.

There are three communities on this eastern side: Balmaha, Rowardennan and Inversnaid. The only road for vehicles runs between Balmaha and Rowardennan, from there on it's on foot or by boat.

Balmaha-Loch Lomond

Balmaha

The village of Balmaha has a variety of restaurants and accommodation and a large car park. A boatyard is operated by the MacFarlane family who deliver the mail throughout the area.

MacFarlane's run a ferry from the jetty to Inchcailloch Island the local beauty spot which has ruins of a former castle and a graveyard in addition to a public barbecue.

Rowardennan

A smaller, but very picturesque place; with beautiful views to the north, from its location at the foot of Ben Lomond. It provides car parking and provisions for walkers, with accommodation in the hotel, caravan and camping site and Rowardennan Lodge in addition to the Youth Hostel.

Inversnaid

Lying to the north of Rowardennan located on the other side of Ben Lomond that towers 3194 ft.

It is accessible from the West Highland Way and a lengthy single track road from Stronachlachar on Loch Katrine.

The hotel has extensive grounds that include Rob Roy's cave. It also provides its own launch, used to transport guests to and from the west bank of the loch. The Cruise Loch Lomond boats call on their routes up and down the loch

Inversnaid Hotel Tel: 01360 660245
Rowardennan Hotel Tel: 01360 870273
Inchmurren Hotel Tel: 01389 850245
MacFarlane Marina Tel: 01360 870214

Primroses

The Trossachs

The Trossachs cover an area of rolling hills, lochs and woodland between Loch Lomond and the Lake of Menteith.

Described in lyrical terms by artists and poets, the journey through the area is made on roads that twist and turn, with great views round most of the bends.

Wildlife abounds. The Rangers within the National Park are knowledgeable and helpful and there are many locations where bird watchers, artists and photographers can view the Park to its best advantage.

From Balloch the journey to the Trossachs is made on the A811 to Drymen.

The direct route is along the A 811 to the junction with the A81 the road to Aberfoyle. The village of Aberfoyle is a tourist resort and the stepping off place for the Trossachs.

Aberfoyle

Because of its associations with Sir Walter Scott the popularity of this village, and indeed the whole area, was established as a resort by the early nineteenth century.

Its importance in the production of slate led to the building of a rail link in the 1880s which, although intended for industrial purposes, was also used for passenger traffic to this popular resort. The railway was closed in 1951 but the holiday traffic continued using the road.

The Woollen Mill in the centre has a museum that includes a film show dedicated to sheep farming and the wool industry. There is also a restaurant and retail shop selling the usual variety of woollen goods and gift items. There is normally an exhibition of birds of prey mounted outside the main doors of the mill.

Elsewhere in the town are antique shops, a tourist office and an assortment of hotels and bed and breakfast establishments.

A recent addition to the park attractions within the Queen Elizabeth Forest just north of Aberfoyle is the 'Go Ape' centre. Cables strung between the trees up to 40 feet above the ground allow transit over a wide area up alongside the birds and amid the treetops.

At the west end of the High Street you can take the single track road to Inversnaid on the east side of Loch Lomond.

Go Ape Centre Tel: 0870 428 5330
Tourist Office Aberfoyle Tel: 08707 200 604
The Scottish Wool Centre. Tel: 01877 382854

The Hills and Lochs

The West Highland Way is the famous road created by General Wade in the great programme of building that took place in the half century after the ill-fated 1715 Jacobite rebellion. The route connects Milngavie with Fort William and was created to allow soldiers to travel quickly into the Highlands to prevent any more uprisings that were thought to have been likely. Though unpaved the road is a passable surface for walkers.

The B 829 road to Inversnaid is single-track with passing places and it runs past Loch Ard, Loch Chon and Loch Arklet on the way to Loch Lomond. This is a picturesque road and although it is used by coaches taking passengers to the hotel, it is not for the faint-hearted.

For those wishing to travel through to Loch Katrine the main A821 goes north from Aberfoyle and up through this most beautiful forest land; hills and valleys covered in woodland, oak, ash birch and pine trees spread around distant views of Loch Drunkie on the way to Loch Katrine and Loch Venacher.

The peaks of the surrounding mountains tower over the green hills. At Loch Achray there is a viewpoint and an information board explaining the location of walks. The Forestry Commission locates these at sites throughout the Trossachs.

Loch Achray is one of the many lochs scattered throughout the Trossachs and like most of these waters fishing is permitted though a licence is normally necessary.

Sir Walter Scott

Loch Katrine

The journey is worth it, Loch Katrine is a reservoir that provides the water supply for most of Glasgow. It is also a beautiful stretch of water deep in the hills, and home of one of the most famous steamers in Scottish waters.

The *Sir Walter Scott* is employed taking passengers around the loch and has done so for the past sixty years. This is the loch that inspired Sir Walter Scott to write *The Lady of the Lake*. Visitors can readily understand why this beautiful location has inspired both writers and poets.

The visitor centre at the head of Loch Katrine provides the usual facilities, parking, toilets and a restaurant; visitors are greeted by an affable gentleman in full Highland dress.

From Loch Katrine the A821 carries on towards Callander following the shores of Loch Achray, through Brig o' Turk, to Loch Venacher on the right. On the left is the entrance to Glen Finglas with a visitor information board detailing of the walks and the beautiful sights of the glen which stretches away to the north and is accessible by footpath only.

From here the road continues on to join the A84 at the Woollen Mill shops at Kilmahog just over a mile west of the town of Callander.

Callander

Lying as it does on the route from Stirling to Fort William and Oban to the north with the Trossachs to the west, Callander is known as the gateway to both the Highlands and the Trossachs

Well known in the 1960s as Tannochbrae, location of the medical practice of Doctors Findlay and Cameron from the TV series *Dr. Findlay's Casebook*, Callander's place in modern history dates from Roman times. The ruins of a first century fort are found to the south of the town.

As recent archaeological finds have indicated, there has been human settlement here for at least 4000 years. Sited where it is, at the meeting of the lush lowlands and the high mountains, Callander is a focal point for visitors.

The town became a favourite resort from the late seventeenth century. Its popularity grew with the visits and subsequent publicity gained through the Lakeland poet William Wordsworth, and of course Sir Walter Scott. The arrival of the railway from Edinburgh to Oban in 1858 made access available to the general public.

The layout of Callander has the feel of a lowland rather than Highland town, with a wide main street lined with small shops, and a central square. The Church in the square is now the tourist office and visitor centre, housing an exhibition based on Rob Roy and the local lands.

Tourist Information Callander Tel 01877 330342
Trossachs Woollen Mill Kilmahog Tel: 01877 331631

Kil, Kin, Aber and Inver

One of the things that you may notice is the number of places prefixed Kil and Kin. Normally Kil is a translation of Cille, an early religious cell or church, thus Kilmore could be either big or great church, or even more confusingly Mary's church (St Mary's), Kilmartin (St Martin's)and Kilmichael (St Michael's). However just to confuse matters even more, Kilmelfort is not St Melfort's church, if such a Saint ever existed. It is actually Kinlochmelfort. Shortened for convenience?

Kin is translated from the Gaelic *ceann* as 'the head of'. Thus Kinlochmelfort means the head of Loch Melfort. Kinlochleven, the head of Loch Leven, and so on.

Names like Aberfeldy, Aberdeen, Aberystwyth,

Aberavon, have a common prefix which means, where two waters join, or a river meets the sea or a loch. Originally Cumbric, the Welsh word translated into Gaelic was *Obair*. The Gaelic word was *Inbhir*. Here in Scotland both words are used, thus place names like Inverness, Invergordon are as acceptable as Aberdeen and Aberfeldy – all refer to the place where a river joins other water. Lochaber means the loch where waters join.

The Waters

Apart from the Atlantic Ocean to the west, the area has a plentiful supply of lochs, ranging from Loch Leven and Loch Linnhe in the north, to the Clydeside lochs and Loch Fyne in the south. Most of the lochs are sea lochs, the major exceptions being Loch Lomond and Loch Awe, home to Kilchurn Castle and reputed to be the longest freshwater loch in Scotland. Dominated in the north by Ben Cruachan, the long narrow loch is scattered with islands down to the village of Ford at the southern end, just a few short miles from the sea. Loch Nell is another fresh water loch alongside the drove road to Kilmore. Of the sea Lochs, Loch Linnhe is important as the route from Mull into the Highlands, past Oban to Fort William and the North and North-East of Scotland. Loch Fyne has for generations been one of the most important Herring and Kipper sources in the west, and it still is an important supplier of, especially smoked, fish and shellfish. The area as a whole is regarded as a sailing boat wonderland, as well it might. Kilmelfort has a Marina as has Crobh Haven. There are moorings at Tarbert, Ardrishaig and Crinan. The waters of Loch Fyne, Loch Long, Gare Loch, Holy Loch and Loch Striven and the Firth of Clyde are a sailing playground in the south. To the north, the sound of Mull, Loch Linnhe, Loch Leven, Loch Etive, and offshore the waters of Corryvreckan and the many channels and sounds provide a challenge no true seaman can resist.

The Clyde Steamers

Mentioned earlier, these ships, developed in the mid nineteenth century, acquired an international reputation for their speed. The private battles between shipping companies in the river trade led to the development of fast vessels using side-wheel paddles as well as turbines. Speeds of 18-21 knots were recorded and expected to enable these ships to compete effectively.

When the war between the states broke out in the USA in 1865, the North mounted a naval blockade of the South to inhibit trade with the rest of the world. In Scotland there was sympathy for the Southern cause, possibly linked to the cotton trade, so sales were treated sympathetically despite being banned by the government. Disguised as sales to the Emperor of China the buyers

The Duchess of Fyfe

from the Confederacy bought fast ships as blockade runners, a blind eye was shown and several of the most famous Clyde steamers sailed across to join the Rebels. A total of eighteen ships from the Clyde took part in the blockade running for the South.

Puffers at Dawn

The Puffers

The coastal towns of Argyll were once dependant on Puffers for the necessities of life. The mountainous country meant that roads were difficult and railways virtually non-existent. The coastal trade was carried out by Puffers. The steam-powered successor to sailing craft became the lifeline for remote communities on island and mainland. With a flat forefoot the Puffers could beach with the tide and float off when unloaded. The trade continued until 1970. Made familiar to the general public through such films as 'The Maggie' and the TV series 'The Vital Spark' these little craft earned their place in the history of the Highlands. The sole remaining operating puffer is the VIC 32 that now carries passengers on tour through the Highlands and Islands where it once carried freight.

Highland Steamboat Holidays Tel: 01545 510232

The Railways

Unlike the railway systems of the regions further north the main railway line has survived in Argyll. The West Highland Railway is now part of the Scotrail system, but it still operates to Oban, Fort William and Mallaig. The trains follow the Clyde shore to Dumbarton, then to Helensburgh, along Gare Loch and Loch Long, then across to Loch Lomond, on its way north to Crianlarich, Tyndrum and thence to Oban or Fort William and Mallaig via the stunning loop across Rannoch Moor. This aspect of the journey is particularly beautiful in the early morning in winter, when the moor is covered with snow. Sadly the line that once ran from Stirling north through Callendar and Balquidder to Crianlarich, has been closed for many years. It was once the link to the Loch Tay town of Killin, famous for its falls and the healing stones of St Fillans.

The Machrihanish railway has of course been superseded by the road across the Mull of Kintyre. This may be more efficient, but the railways of the past carried a cachet of romance that has never been replaced.